BETWEEN THE SHADOWS

A Memoir of a Wartime Childhood

By Frima Laub

Illustrated by Elizabeth Uhlig

Marble House Editions

Published by Marble House Editions
96-09 66th Avenue (Suite 1D)
Rego Park, NY 11374

Copyright © 2008 by Frima Laub
All rights reserved

No part of this publication may be reproduced, stored in, or introduced into a retrieval system, or transmitted in any form or by any means (electronic, mechanical, photocopying, recording, or otherwise) without the prior written permission of both the copyright owner and the above publisher of this book.

Library of Congress Cataloguing-in-Publication Data

Laub, Frima

Between the Shadows/by Frima Laub

Summary: The true story of a Jewish child who survived on her own when she was left behind during World War II.

ISBN 978-0-9815345-2-7
Library of Congress Catalog Card Number
2008935145
Printed in China

This book is dedicated to the memory of my Papa and the 1.5 million children who perished in the Holocaust.

TABLE OF CONTENTS

Prologue
1. The Trouble Begins
2. The First Miracle
3. Mama's Plan
4. Help From a Neighbor
5. Left Behind
6. Finding My Own Way
7. A New Identity
8. Surviving Alone
9. Out of Poland
10. Reunion
11. The War Ends
12. The Return
13. We Start Over
14. Leaving Europe
Epilogue

PROLOGUE

In 1933, when Adolf Hitler came to power in Germany, Europe began to experience the destruction of its entire Jewish community. Millions of people were persecuted, only for being Jewish. Victims lost their families, homes and homelands during the harsh years of war that followed, 1939-1945. This story gives special attention to the children, the innocent and terrified youngsters who were pursued, captured and often exterminated along with other unfortunate citizens, all of them caught in Germany's reign of terror.

Between the Shadows *is the story of how one child, alone and defenseless, survived by virtue of her own will, inner strength, and the benevolence of a few righteous people.*

1. THE TROUBLE BEGINS

I was only five and a half years old when the darkness came over Poland. I remember that it was like a giant shadow that suddenly covered everything around us with sadness and fear.

Up until then, Mama, Papa, Jeannie, and I had been living a cozy, comfortable life. Our elegant house, which stood majestically on a shady street in town, was always filled with the wonderful smell of Mama's cooking. There was lively company and plenty of music. And at night, Papa would sing me, little Feema, to sleep as I sat on his lap with Kitzi, my fluffy grey cat.

But then the news broke out that German soldiers, Nazis, were coming to our town. Mama and Papa knew that this would be the end of our cherished way of life.

We had already heard the terrible stories about what was happening in other parts of Europe. The day the news came, all the Jewish families started to leave town any way they could, carrying only small necessities. Most people were walking.

The day before we left, Mama had to cancel delivery of the new piano Papa had ordered for me. Just the year before, when I was four and a half, I was already playing quite well. Such luxuries and niceties of life would have to wait now.

Mama had some valuable pieces of jewelry and other small, precious items, treasures that would never be safe if the Nazis knew about them. Some of these objects had belonged to my grandmother and great grandmother; they were family heirlooms that Mama did not want to risk losing. As a safety measure, she wrapped them carefully and put them in a large lidded jar. Then she dug a hole in the front yard near the lilac tree and buried that jar, hoping that one day she might retrieve it from its hiding place.

Then we left too, in our horse and buggy, and traveled eastward toward Belarus. None of us knew if we would ever see our homes again.

My brother David was going to school somewhere out beyond the borders of Poland. We had lost contact with him and it would be a long time before we would know where he was or what had happened to him. We did not even know what would happen to us!

On our way to Belarus we heard that we were surrounded. The soldiers had caught up with us and there was no sense in trying to run away. In despair, we all turned back.

When we returned to our town, we learned that the house we had lived in was no longer ours. All Jewish homes and shops had been seized by the Nazis. Entire families were sent to live in the ghetto, a neighborhood where Jews were confined. We were forced to share an apartment with another family. It was very crowded, but no one was allowed to leave!

We tried to have as normal a life as possible, keeping our Jewish traditions and some feeling of community. But little by little, every bit of the life we had known was eroding. People we loved were disappearing, either because they were arrested by the Nazis or simply because there was not enough food for all the people in the ghetto. Families were split apart, babies and old people died, and darkness was in the air all the time.

My nine year-old cousin Isac and his family were in the ghetto with us. Isac and I became close, almost like a very young boyfriend and girlfriend. We passed the long, fear-filled days by going for walks together around the ghetto. As we strolled along, Isac used to sing a little song to me. In English it would go something like this:

Let go of all your cares,

Just keep close to your dream.

You and I will stay together

As a perfect team.

Someday you'll be my angel for life,

And in my dreams my beautiful wife.

And as he sang, we used to imagine the days to come and how we would still be together. How could we have known that none of this would happen? Poor Isac! Only later, much later, would I have time to think about what happened to this precious companion and the rest of his family.

* * *

As if things could not get worse, one day Papa was taken away and made to work as a Polish interpreter for the Germans. How quickly our lives had changed.

Early one morning not long after that, we awoke to the harsh screaming of German soldiers. "Get out!" they shouted, as they forced us from our one-room apartment and rounded us up in the street. Big, threatening dogs were barking fiercely and people were running in all directions. I grabbed my doll, Kukla, and ran too, but I did not know where we were going. *How would Papa find us?* I thought.

2. THE FIRST MIRACLE

Suddenly, all the noise stopped. We found ourselves marching out of the ghetto in a silent, sad line, toward the very edges of town and into the forest. We had heard about how people were taken into the forest and never returned, and we were scared.

A soft drizzle came down upon us, as if the sky were weeping. Deep in the forest, people had to take off most of their clothing and leave it in an enormous pile. The discarded clothing spoke of the people who had been there before us. Kukla was left there, too.

In the crowd of terrified people I saw Isac and his parents and other faces I knew from the ghetto. No one said anything. We just marched along as we were told to. *What was going to happen to all of us?*

As we walked, I heard Mama say softly, "Children, this would be a good time for G-d to hear us." Suddenly, a black cat crossed our path. Being superstitious, Mama believed that we had to be headed for certain death. Quietly, she told us to say the *Shemah Yisroel!*, our prayer of faith and devotion to G-d, in the hope that He would save us. We looked up toward heaven in prayer. And just then, the sun came out.

Mama knew she had to do something. She stepped out of the line and approached the guard. "We do not belong here!" she said. "We are Ukrainian, not Jewish!" she lied.

The guard looked at us suspiciously. Did he know Mama was lying? We will never know, but this was our first miracle: suddenly our

path was reversed and we were walked back to town under the watchful eye of a Ukrainian guard.

As we were walking, we could not help but see the lines of Jewish people headed in the direction of the forest. We knew what awaited them there, and a profound sadness was upon us. Mama let out a sigh, and then without thinking, she said, "Oy," as she felt the deep despair about what was happening. This little word, a Jewish word, was to be our undoing.

When we got to town, Mama turned to the guard who had been walking alongside us. "Thank you," she said, "for bringing us back. Because of you we were not stopped by soldiers."

"Don't thank me," he said with a sneer. "You are not going anywhere. You are *Jews*, and I am taking you to the police station."

At the police station we were asked many questions by stern and pitiless men in uniforms. I was terribly frightened, but I would not show it. I just stuck with Mama's story: we were Ukrainian, not Jewish.

Unable to determine the truth about us, the police put us in a jail cell. We did not know how long we would be kept there or what would happen to us next. Mama knew we just had to escape soon and she was determined to get us out.

3. MAMA'S PLAN

For four days and four nights, Mama observed the jail guards' routine. Then one morning, at the first light of dawn, when the guards' backs were turned, like stealthy cats, we tiptoed out of the jail cell, first I, then Mama, then Jeannie.

And so began the time in our lives when we would be forever hiding, escaping and running: hiding from soldiers, fleeing quickly from our refuge and running to the next safe place. We even spent one night in a public toilet, a crude, cold structure with little protection.

Every day we ran between the buildings and shadows, making our way to each new hiding place. We concealed ourselves in dark corners of the town and slipped carefully from one place to the next, trying to be invisible.

Finally one day at dusk we reached the home of our friend Mr. Petrov. He understood the danger we were in and offered to hide us in his cellar for the night. It was a dark, dank room filled with rats and rotten potatoes, but we did not mind. We knew we had been very lucky and we were grateful to be safe. Mama had been so brave. She would have to be brave for a long time to come, as would I.

The next morning we left that house and continued walking until we reached the ghetto. We found Papa there. He was overjoyed to see us, but sad to tell us that our relatives, including my dear cousin Isac, had not returned from the forest, as we had.

The situation in all of Poland had worsened very quickly and now no one was safe. Nobody knew what would happen next, for in the ghetto we had no communication with the outside world. We just had to wait and see what fate had in store for us.

It was then that I came down with a mysterious ailment. It might have been chicken pox, measles, or some other childhood disease. It itched horribly and was definitely contagious. There was no hospital or any doctor for Jewish people. No one could know about this because if the Nazis discovered an ill child among the Jewish population, it would be the end of me.

Mama wanted me to live. I had to hide, but where could I go and not arouse suspicion? Somehow, Mama found a Gentile couple who lived outside the ghetto and asked if I could stay with them. Being childless, they were willing to take care of me. They actually hoped to adopt me and keep me forever. We were lucky to find someone we could trust.

The next night, Mama smuggled me out of the ghetto, carrying me because I was too weak and too sick to walk. She took me to Mr. and Mrs. Ivanov, two hardworking people who lived in a small apartment. When Mama left me, she may not have known that she would ever see me again, but she was glad that I was safe, at least for the moment.

The Ivanovs set up a little cot for me to sleep on and strung up a curtain so that we could each have some privacy. Every night, Mrs. Ivanov washed me down and smeared cream all over me to stop the itching. Then to make sure I didn't scratch the red spots, she would bind me up in cloth. In the morning before leaving for work, Mr. Ivanov set out some food for me.

I stayed alone in the apartment all day, hiding, waiting, and healing from my illness.

The Ivanovs worked long hours and came home tired, but they were never too tired to care for me. They treated me as though I were their own child, and I think now that they must have wished I felt that way about them. But I didn't. I saw their goodness and knew they were saving my life, but despite the kindness I had been shown, I missed my family in the ghetto.

About three weeks later, I knew I had recovered and decided to leave. The itching had stopped and the redness was gone. When Mr. and Mrs. Ivanov left for work, I got dressed. Opening the door, I saw the shining sun and the blue sky. I simply walked out, closing the door behind me.

Although I did not know where the Ivanovs lived or where I had been staying, somehow I found my way back to the ghetto. As I walked through the streets, I saw soldiers and just hoped that I could make it safely to our apartment. I did not know then that this was a preview of what I would go through many times in the days to come.

When I arrived, my mother was shocked

but happy to see me. I explained to her that I did not want to stay with the Ivanovs anymore. They had treated me well, but I was homesick for her and the rest of the family. Mama understood. She was concerned, though, that the Ivanovs would be worried when they came home and found me missing. But she could not attend to that problem now. Someday, when all of this mess was over, we would find these people and thank them for all they had done.

* * *

We knew that it was only a matter of time before we came face to face with danger again, and now that we were all together, we had to escape from the ghetto. But how? The ghetto was surrounded by barbed wire. Mama said we had no choice and she made a plan. We would crawl under the barbed wire at night. First I would go, followed by Jeannie and Mama, then Papa. I did not want Papa to be last. I was afraid I would never see him again.

That night, quietly and barely breathing, we crawled out, squeezing our bodies under the deadly wire. When the three of us were on the other side, we waited nervously for Papa. Then we heard him call to us. "I will come later!" he whispered, but his voice sounded uncertain. We learned later, much later, that Papa did not make it out of the ghetto, as we had hoped.

4. HELP FROM A NEIGHBOR

Now we had to find a new hideout. We fled back to our hometown, to a nearby farm that had a barn. There, another kind neighbor, Mrs. Kuzlov, offered to let us stay in her hayloft.

Up in the hayloft, day after day, we waited, terrified. Every morning, Mrs. Kuzlov crept out of her house to bring us food. We had to keep very still and hoped that our hiding place would not be discovered. And for a little while, we felt safe and were so grateful to this woman who was risking her life to save ours.

But one morning we heard her voice desperately calling out to us. "Save yourselves! Save yourselves!" she shouted, and we knew that soldiers had found out about us. Quickly, so quickly, Mama broke through the barn's wooden slats. We all jumped to the ground and ran to another neighbor's house. I do not know what became of the brave Mrs. Kuzlov who hid us.

5. LEFT BEHIND

Mama knew that to really be safe, we would have to get out of Poland altogether. But as Jews, we could not travel. We could not even let anyone know we existed! A kindhearted priest in town was helping people get false identification papers, and he offered to help us too. We were very lucky because without

these papers, we could not have gone anywhere.

Once we had our precious documents, the question was, where would we go now? Mama told me her plan. "I have arranged for Jeannie and me to be smuggled into Romania, to a ghetto there."

I was astonished. "What about me?" I asked.

"You cannot come now, my child. Winter is here and I don't think you will survive this trip. You will freeze. I am leaving you here with Mrs. Podloska, and in the spring, our friend Vladislav will come for you and bring you to me in Romania."

Tears wanted to come but I did not let them. Instead I said, "Mama, how my head hurts!" I did not really understand why I could not go too.

Mama gave me some money, kissed me and left me there with Mrs. Podloska, who hid me in her home, letting me sleep on a bench in her little pantry. At night, I used to cover my face with a blanket but I could still

feel mice crawling all over me.

Mrs. Podloska had a dog, too, who was a kind companion to me in my loneliness. She slept in a cubbyhole under the house.

Of course, Mama had given Mrs. Podloska something for her kindness – money and

some precious items from our house – a Persian rug and what little jewelry she had taken when we left our house. What else could she do? She hoped these valuable objects would be adequate payment for keeping me hidden until the spring.

Mrs. Podloska could not do much for me other than feed me and let me hide there. I was grateful for this, but there was no way for me to wash or have clean clothes. And so it did not take long before my head and body became infested with lice. They were everywhere – in my hair, on my skin, in my clothes. They crawled all over me, making me scratch and scratch until my scalp bled. The itching was unbearable.

Sometimes I used to creep under the dining room table and, hidden by the long, draping tablecloth, I would comb the tiny creatures out of my hair, letting them fall into a scarf on my lap. Then I would shake that scarf out the window, tossing the lice into the air. But it was no use. The bugs were multiplying faster than I could get rid of them.

As horrible as it sounds, the lice infestation

was among the least of my problems because only two weeks later Mrs. Podloska said to me, "Feema, you have to leave. It is not safe for me to have you here. The Nazis are going from house to house looking for Jews, and if they find you, it will be the end for both you and me."

I understood. It would just be one more time that I would have to find a new hiding place. *Where will I go?* I thought.

6. FINDING MY OWN WAY

I went out into the street. Snow was falling gently. I did not know what to do next, so I began to walk. By and by, I found myself on the outskirts of town. I remembered that our family had some friends there, and I went to their house and knocked. The familiar face of Mrs. Rozov appeared at the door. "Feema!" she said. "What are you doing here? Where are your parents?"

"Everyone is dead," I replied, because I could not think of anything else to say. I hoped she would feel sorry for me and take me in.

Mrs. Rozov looked at me with sadness. "Come in," she whispered, and made a sign for me to be very quiet. We walked silently down a long hallway. "You must not make a sound," she warned me. "And no one can

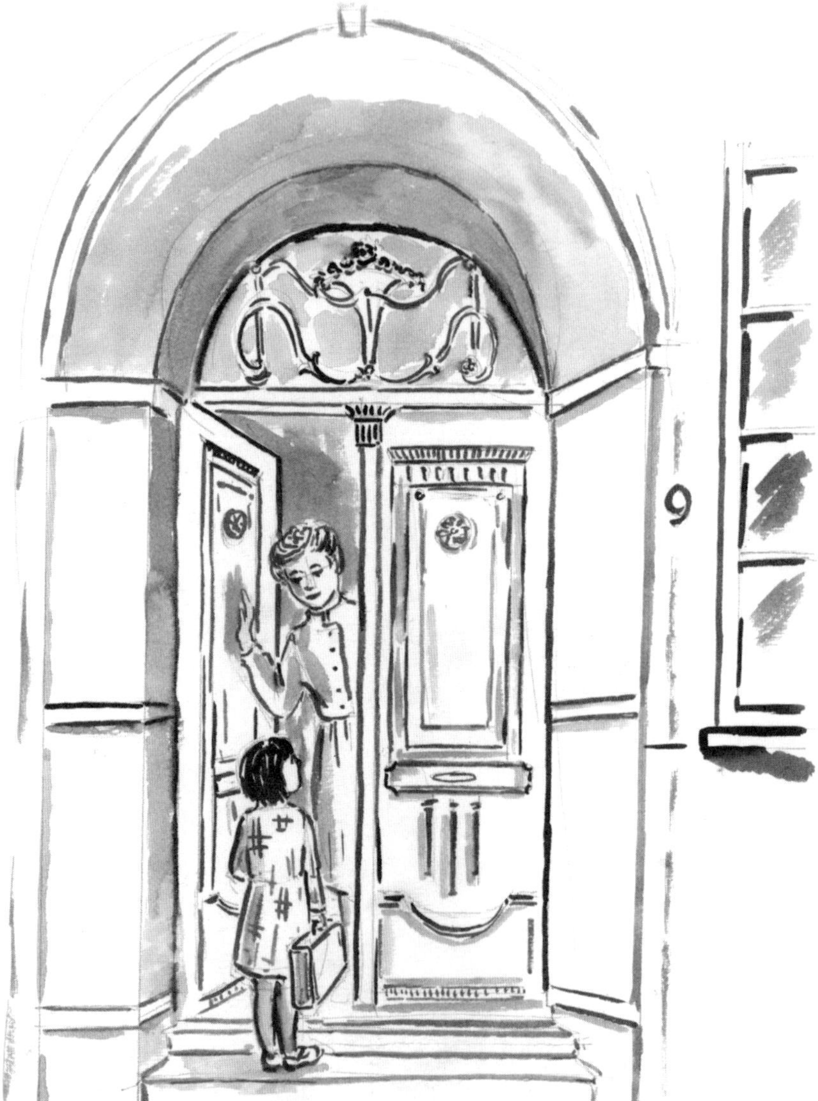
9

know that you are here." I understood. I was getting used to trying to be invisible.

Mrs. Rozov saw right away that I was being eaten alive by lice! She took me into her garage and said, "Feema, take off these filthy clothes! You poor little girl – you need a bath!" Then she brought me inside and had me step into the tub. It felt good to be surrounded by hot, soapy water.

Mrs. Rozov looked at my little body, which was covered with scratch marks. "You will feel better soon, Feema," she sighed. "I will have to cut your hair, though. That is the only way your scalp will heal." I nodded, and was relieved that soon the itching might stop.

After the bath, Mrs. Rozov hung my clothes outside in the freezing air to kill the lice. There was no other way, for these were the only clothes I had. She gave me one of her nightgowns to wear. How good it was to be clean and safe, sitting near the fireplace in Mrs. Rozov's bedroom, having milk and bread.

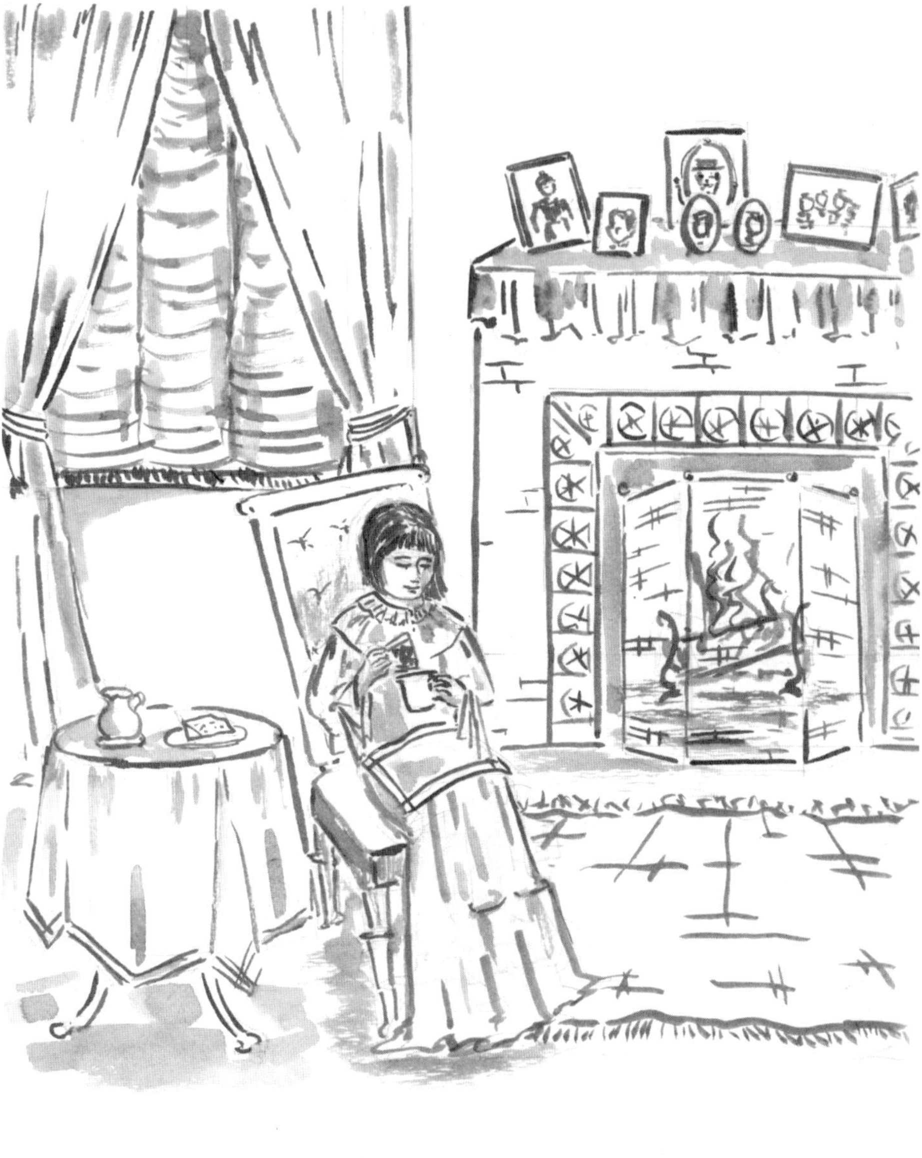

I stayed there for one week, hiding. But one day, like the others before her, Mrs. Rozov came to me and said, "Feema, you have to leave. I cannot keep you here any longer because it is not safe for me." How many times I had heard this! I knew that this good woman had tried to help me, but now her own life was in danger, as it was for anyone protecting Jews.

And at that moment, I knew that from now on, I was going to have to survive on my own. No one was going to hide me anymore. It was also clear now, that no one, no one at all, could learn that I was Jewish. I left that house and once again began to walk the streets, with no destination.

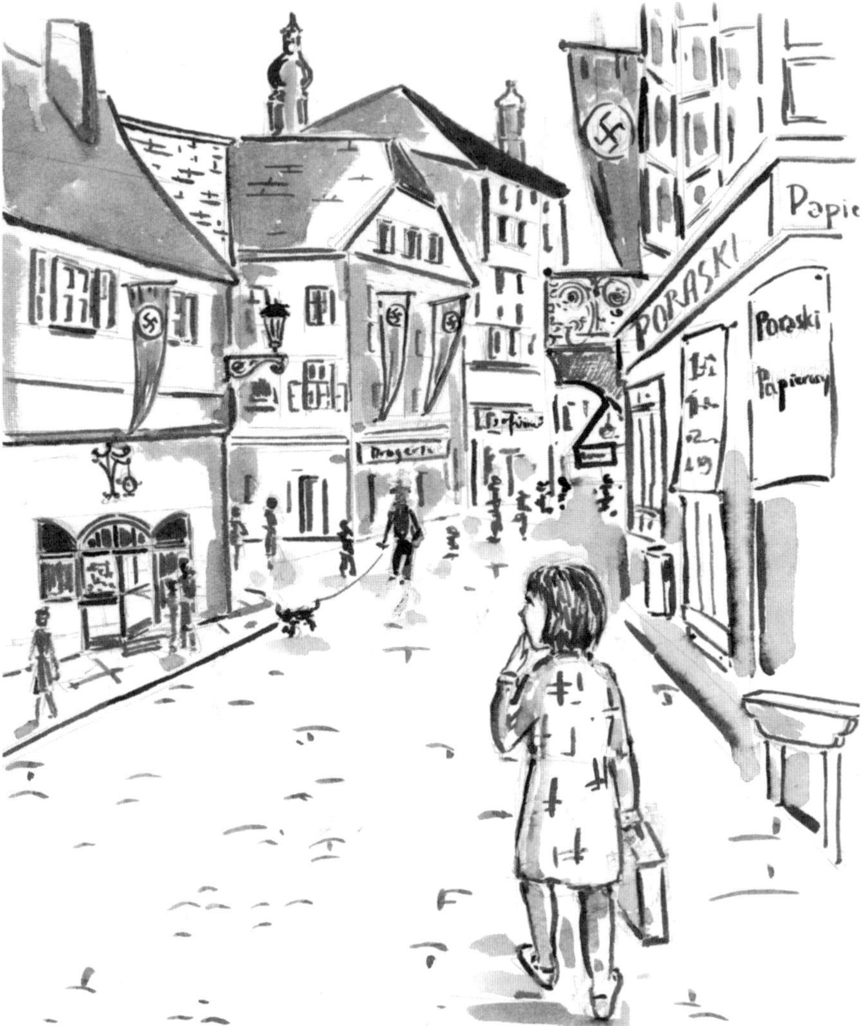
Papie
PORASKI
Poraski

7. A NEW IDENTITY

Passing a shop that sold religious items and jewelry, I saw many gold and silver crosses and medals on display in the window. It was clear what I had to do. I walked in, and with all of the money Mama had given me, I bought a large silver cross on a chain. Placing it around my neck, I made a silent decision: *From now on, if anyone asks, I will say I'm a Gentile girl named Olga.* I had to change my identity.

It was important to wear the cross so that everyone could see it because I did not want to be stopped for interrogation. I remembered well how, when we were in jail, I was made to sit on the lap of a Nazi interrogator. He was sure that he would get me to tell the truth about whether or not we were Jews or Ukrainians. Well, he failed.

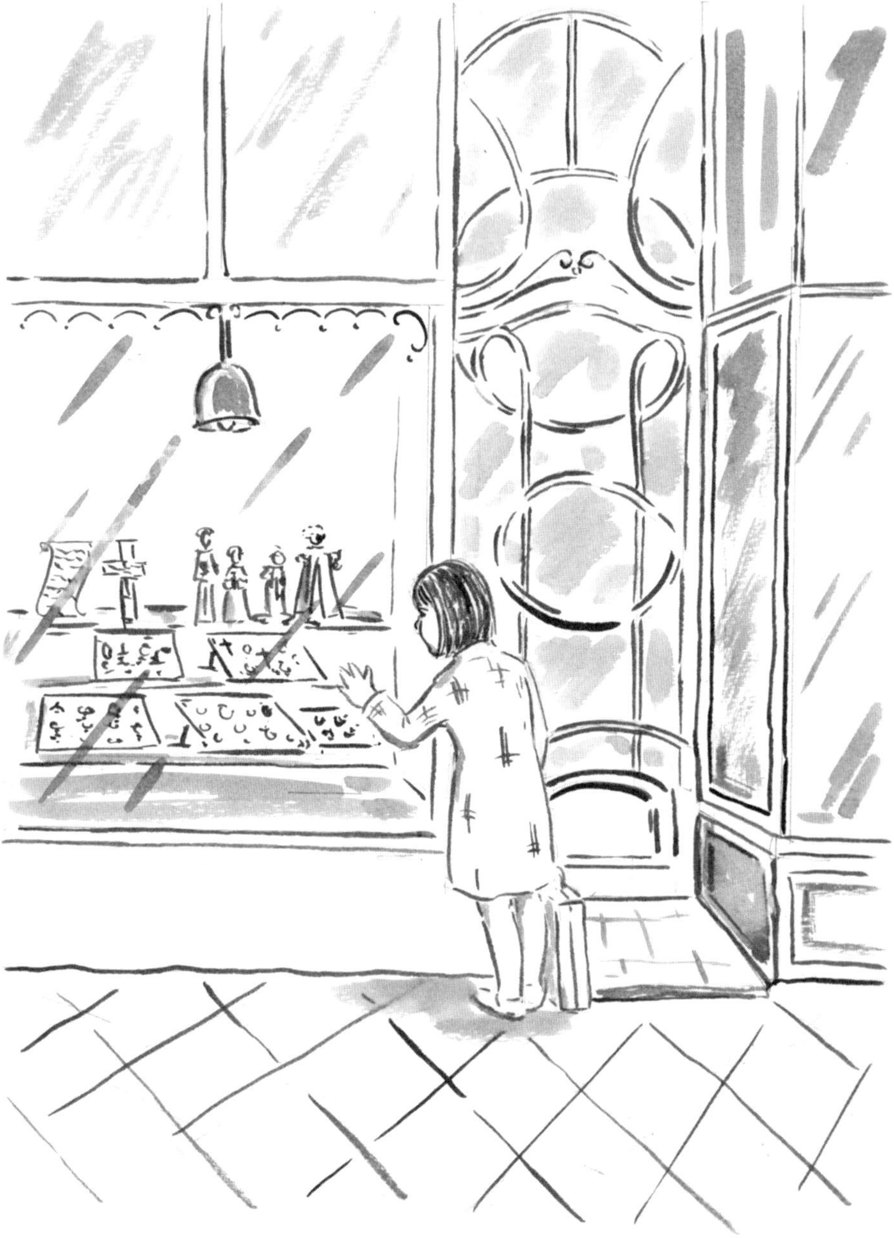

I knew that if I was going to be alone for the whole winter, I would have to live among the people of this town unseen. I would have to find food and shelter, and stay warm and alive until springtime when I could join my mother in Romania. Until that time, I planned to walk and walk all over town, hoping not to be noticed or recognized.

That day, I went up and down each street, round and round each corner, hour after hour. I just kept walking. As dusk started to fall upon the city, I wondered where I would stay for the night. Where could I go where I would be invisible and safe? Then I thought of the house where I had stayed in the pantry and remembered the dog that slept in the cubbyhole. I walked back to that part of town, slipping between the trees and shadows, and by nightfall I found the place. I slid my small body into the crawl space under the house. The familiar dog was there, but she did not bark. I think she knew I was afraid. I lay my head on her soft fur. We slept side by side, and she kept me warm.

I took off the cross and got ready to say my evening prayer. I had not forgotten what I learned at home, and before lying down to rest, I said the *Kriyat Shemah al Hamitah,* a prayer for safety and protection against the dangers of the night. I may have been separated from my family, but I would still carry out the rituals that were always a part of our lives in better times.

When I awoke very early the next day, I said the morning prayer, *Mode Ani,* and gratefully thanked G-d for blessing me with another day. I shook off whatever scraps of dirt were clinging to my clothing, put on the cross so that it would be visible, and started walking the streets. I left my hiding place just as the sun was rising, and although I had nowhere to go and little to hope for, I did hold on to the thought that in the spring I would be reunited with my mother.

Each day I chose a different part of town to walk in so that no one would see me too often. I suppose people did see me, but no one knew who I was. Because my money had run out, I had to get food from good-hearted people in town. But sometimes all I had to eat was snow.

On one especially cold day I took a long walk back to Mr. Petrov's house where I had hidden in the cellar with Mama and Jeannie. I was just so hungry, and remembering Mr. Petrov's kindness, I wondered if he would give me something to eat.

By now the city had been emptied of Jews, so when Mr. Petrov saw me at his front door, he was surprised. "Feema!" he said, "What are you doing walking around all alone?" I did not answer. He stepped aside and let me in. "Are you hungry?" he asked. I nodded yes.

He sat me at a table and went into the kitchen. Very quickly, he brought out a glass of milk and a plate of food and set them both before me. I looked down at the plate. There was a piece of black bread and a little slice of pork. The bread looked fine, but being Jewish, I could not eat the pork. I knew Mr. Petrov meant well; he probably did not know about this rule. But in spite of the suffering I was enduring, I had not forgotten who I was and where I had come from, and I *could* not and *would* not eat pork.

I tasted the bread and milk. It was so good! I smiled at Mr. Petrov, who looked concerned. "Feematchka," he said affectionately, "take a bite of the meat. It's cold outside and it will help you keep warm."

I didn't want to hurt this man's feelings. *That* would be just as much of a sin as eating pork. I knew he was trying to help me. "Mr. Petrov," I said, "thank you so much, but what I really like is this bread and milk. I am just fine with this."

He looked confused. "Are you sure, my dear?"

"Yes," I said, gracefully refusing once again.

I finished my little meal, thanked Mr. Petrov and got up to leave. Just before I walked out the door, he gave me another piece of bread to put in my pocket. He did not know where I was going. Neither did I. But for the moment, I was not hungry anymore.

It was not always possible to go to neighbors and ask for food. I did not want anyone to become suspicious and of course, there were days with no food at all. One rainy afternoon, when I could not endure the cold and emptiness anymore, I stopped to look in the big glass window of a restaurant. I could see that it was warm inside and many people were eating. There was a vacant stool at the counter, next to a man. I walked in, taking that seat. The man was enjoying a bowl of potato soup, fragrant with onions and carrots. It looked so delicious. I knew I had no money, but still I told the waitress I wanted a bowl of that soup.

The steaming plate arrived and I took the first spoonful. It tasted like heaven. I ate it very quickly and felt warm and satisfied. But when the waitress brought me the check, I just stared at it and started to cry. How would I pay it? I had spent my money on the cross.

The man in the next seat looked down at me. Then saying nothing, he took the check from my hands and nodded. He was one more person, this time a nameless one, who showed me kindness. I ran out of the restaurant in tears.

This is how I lived for six months, learning to survive. I found ways to get food and different places to sleep. Many times I slept in the ruins of an old house, under the bleak, open sky. It was often so cold that I had to blow my warm breath into my sweater to keep from freezing...

8. SURVIVING ALONE

One day I wandered back to the neighborhood where I had lived with my family. That all seemed so long ago now. I saw that our beautiful house had been taken over by the Nazis and was being used as a kind of headquarters. To my surprise, Kitzi was still there, and she recognized me! But I could not let anyone see that, so I just kept walking. There were soldiers everywhere.

Kitzi followed me from behind, mewing gently. Suddenly, a shot rang out and then there was silence. I knew that Kitzi was dead. I stared straight ahead and kept going, swallowing my tears. I shall never know if that shot was meant for me or my cat …

Next I went to the place where my father had worked and stood outside the building, hoping to see him come out. I waited there

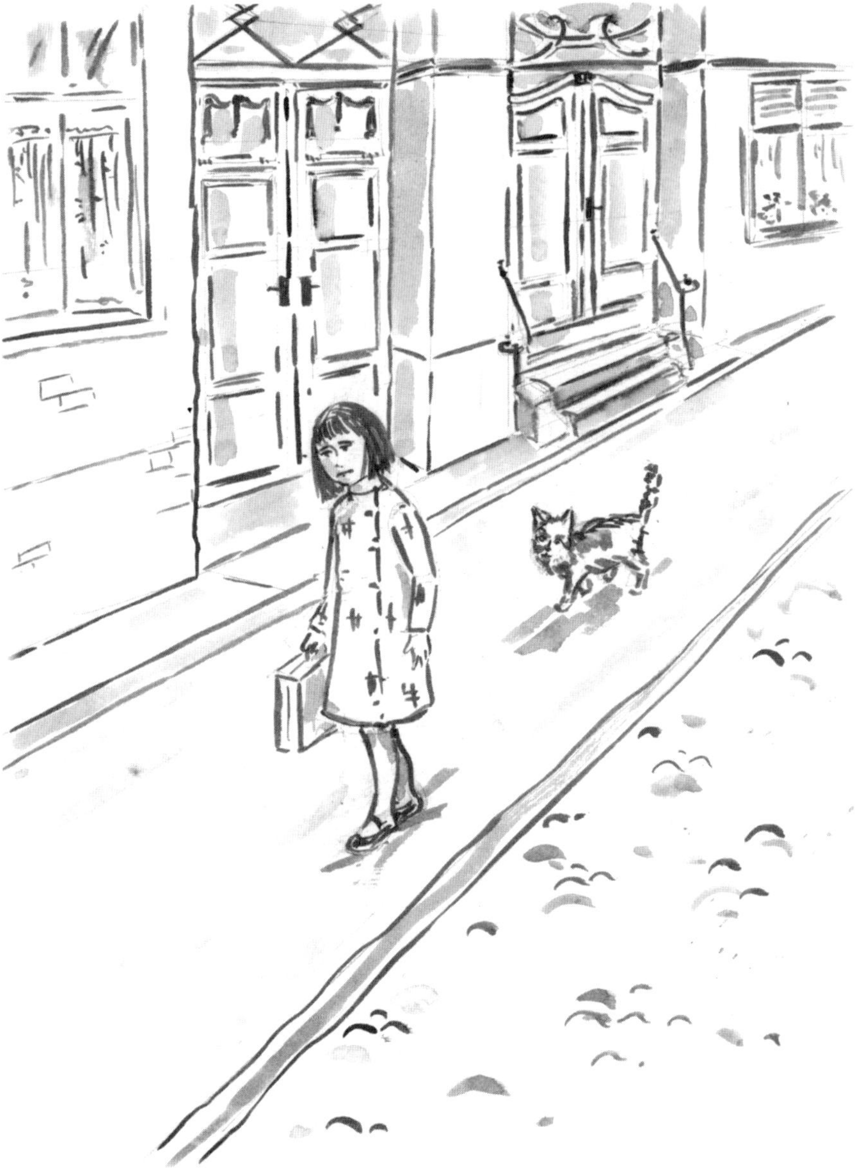

all day, until the shadows darkened the street. Then a man came out of the building and saw me standing there shivering. "Little girl, what are you doing here all by yourself?" he asked kindly.

"I am waiting for my Papa," I replied.

The man took pity on me. "Everyone has gone home, little one. There is no one in the building. I don't think you will see your Papa tonight."

He took me to his house and told his wife to let me sleep on the couch. It was so good to be indoors where it was warm! But in the morning, before anyone was awake, I left.

Months went by and finally it was April, the beginning of spring. Somehow, I had withstood the cold, brutal winter on my own. I hoped that Vladislav, who had smuggled Mama and Jeannie out of Poland, would be coming back to find me. Mama had promised he would. I returned to the house where I had slept in the tiny pantry and waited behind it for Vladislav to come and get me.

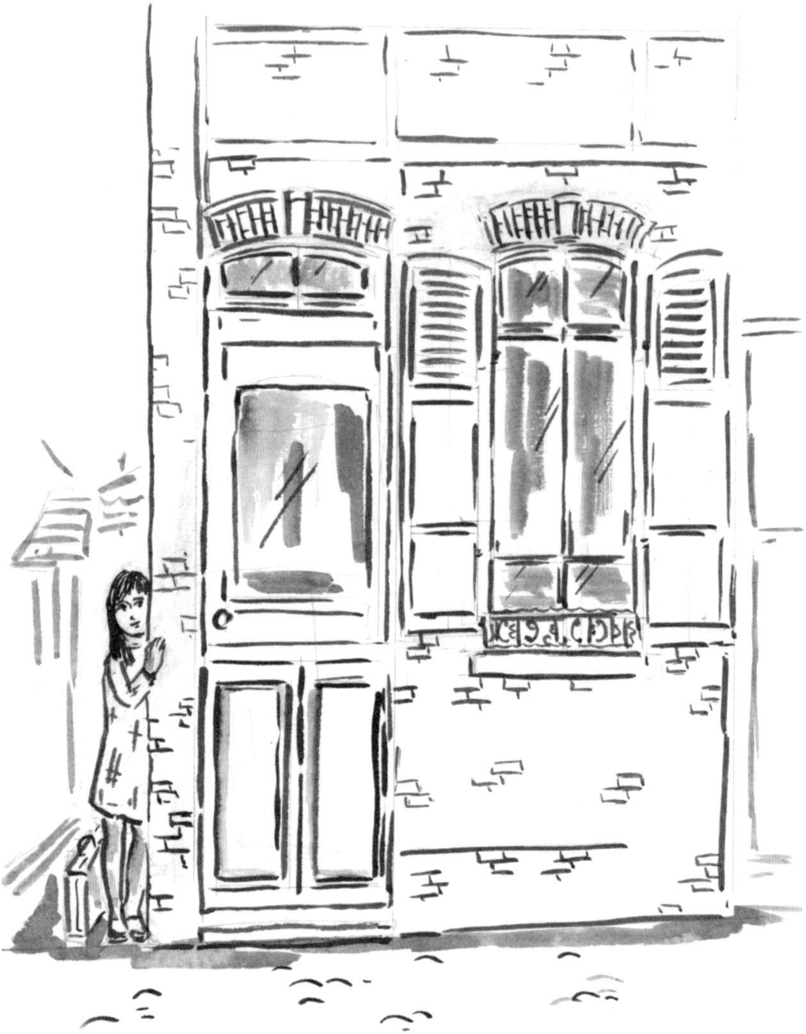

9. OUT OF POLAND

One day soon after that, I saw Vladislav in the street. He *had* come back to take me to Romania! I did not tell him that all these months I had not been in the house where Mama left me. Would he, or anyone, ever believe I had lived alone and unprotected on the city streets?

Vladislav was taking another girl to Romania, too. That evening, moving quickly through the darkness, he put the two of us onto the open car of a train. We traveled all night long across the flat Polish landscape, huddling together to keep warm.

In the early morning, we heard a door open and a German soldier came out. We were both terrified, but my traveling companion, like me, had gotten used to not showing it. "Where are you going?" the soldier asked sternly.

"To see our mother," we replied, pretending to be sisters.

The soldier made a quick motion and suddenly the train came to a halt. He ordered us to get off and we found ourselves standing in the muddy field below. We looked up at the cruel face and began to cry and plead desperately. Some small part of the soldier must have felt sorry for us because he allowed us to climb aboard again.

When the train arrived in Romania, Vladislav took me to the ghetto. I was bursting with excitement at the thought of being reunited with my mother and sister. But my excitement was soon to dissolve, for I quickly learned that Mama and Jeannie were not there! They had left the ghetto months before so that Mama could save money to pay for my passage. *Had I come all this way for nothing? How would I find Mama and Jeannie now?*

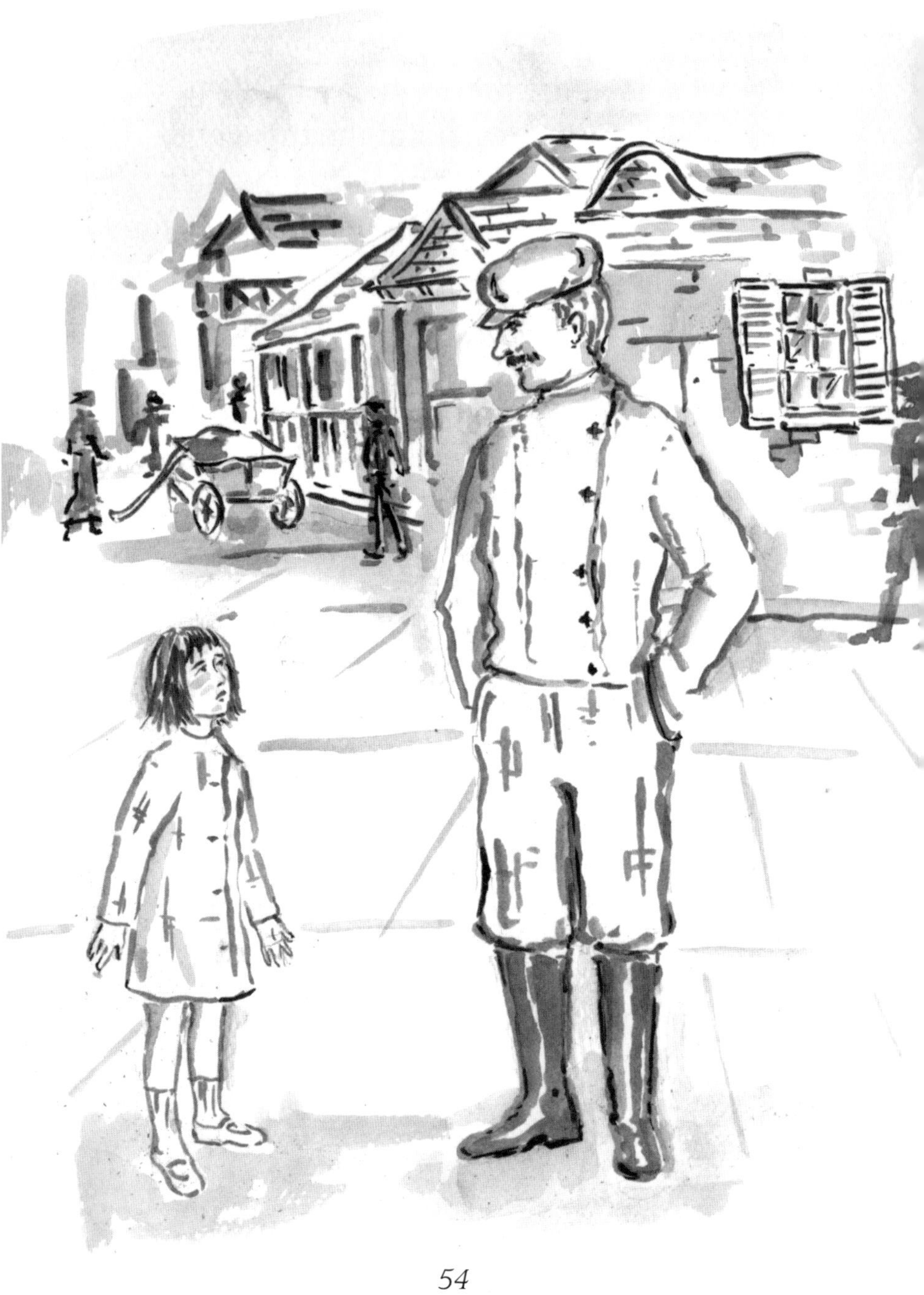

10. REUNION

Vladislav was disappointed. He was expecting Mama to pay him for rescuing me, and now she was not here! Was he going to take me back to Poland? No. Instead, he took me to see the man who was in charge of the ghetto. "Where is my mother?" I asked him with tears in my eyes.

"Who is your mother?" he asked. When I told him Mama's name, he said that she had gone to another town. "Go and find her there," he advised.

But how would I get there? Once again, I was lucky. In the ghetto there was a man who had a horse and buggy. He made a daily trip to the town where Mama and Jeannie were staying, and he offered to take me there!

I got into the buggy with three Jewish men who were also trying to find their families. We rode through the open countryside, bumping along together. Suddenly, we were stopped by soldiers. Horrified, I watched them force the three tattered travelers off the buggy. *They are not going to get me*, I thought. *Not now, when I have come so far and gone through so much.* And before the soldiers could even see me, I jumped off the buggy and ran into the field. Hiding myself in a haystack, I peered out into the countryside.

How long would I have to hide here? Day turned into night and I stayed in my secret place. I prayed to G-d. *Where am I? What shall I do? Where shall I go?* And some time later, I fell asleep...

In the morning, I awoke to the sound of horses. Were soldiers coming for me? I peeked out of the haystack. It was the same horse and buggy I had traveled in the day before! I jumped out into the open field, ran to the buggy and jumped on as the horse kept trotting.

Finally we reached the next village, and the driver stopped the horse in the big town square. Word must have spread quickly that little Feema was in Romania, because right away, I saw Jeannie coming to meet me. Then Mama came running too, and was soon covering me with hugs and kisses. It was hard to believe that we were together again. It was another miracle!

11. THE WAR ENDS

Mama looked down at me and smiled. It was so good to see her blue eyes again. Then she gently touched the cross around my neck. I could see that she was confused. "What is this, my child?" she asked.

"Mama," I said, "I only wanted to live."

She understood, but when the village priest came to welcome me, Mama took the cross off my neck and gave it to him as a gift.

Mama and Jeannie took me to the farm where they had been living. Another mother and daughter were staying there with them. Everyone worked on the farm, digging for potatoes and filling sacks to be taken to the warehouse. This is how they had survived the winter. And now I could help too.

The farmer did not tell the neighbors we were Jewish. He told them we were his family. For a whole day of work, he gave us a loaf of black bread. How wonderful it tasted, and how grateful we were! We stayed peacefully on the farm for two years.

12. THE RETURN

It was luck, generous people, and the help of G-d that had seen us through our ordeal, and now another miracle came our way. The very day before the German soldiers were due to arrive in our town, Russian soldiers got there first. The war was ending and we knew we had been saved. Now we could go home.

We journeyed back by train and on foot. The trip took two long days with no food. When we arrived in town, we learned that the place we had called home was not even Poland anymore! The war had changed the borders, and we now lived in the Ukraine. But the house would be ours again, and we were going back to it.

When we got there, we found our house empty and badly damaged from the war. But we were more fortunate than other people whose houses were taken over by other families, or simply destroyed.

When the moment was right, Mama dug into the earth beneath the lilac tree, hoping to find that jar with the prized possessions, which she had buried years before. She dug and dug, but found nothing. Gone, all gone. Grandmother's pins and rings, Great-grandmother's pearls, Grandfather's watch. Lost. Someone must have seen Mama bury that jar and came to steal it while we were away.

But these jewels were among the smallest treasures we had lost. Gone were our friends, our neighbors, our family members, and our way of life. Gone was our culture, our music, our community with its traditions.

Mama did not look back. Instead, she was determined to make a home for us again, one that was livable. With her own hands, she fixed and painted our house and we began our life anew.

* * *

Everything had changed. Germany had lost

the war and those Nazis who had been our oppressors were now prisoners. They were paraded through the city as an act of humiliation, their hands shackled behind their backs and their heads bent in shame. Their goal of conquering the world had been defeated.

Where were their terrifying uniforms, their guns, their fierce dogs? Where were their haughty, sneering faces, their might, and their threatening looks? All were gone with the defeat that Germany suffered. Now they were dressed in dull, grey rags and their faces were zombie-like as they walked past crowds of jeering, applauding onlookers. Now *we* were the ones to watch *them* as they plodded along with no future, just as we had not had a future when they led us into forests and prison camps.

During those years of suffering, and while I watched my loved ones suffer, I had always had this thought: *If, when this war ends, I ever see a Nazi and can hurt him, I **will**!* But that is not what I felt that day as I watched the humbled prisoners. No, *that* day, when I finally had the chance to jeer and sneer as other people were doing, I began to cry. Why? I looked at those men and I felt sorry for them. I saw them as *people*, not soldiers, for they were not soldiers anymore. They were just men whose lives were now broken, men who had believed in an idea that had been crushed.

Now they were just bedraggled prisoners who might never see their families again. *Do they have children waiting at home?* I wondered. *Will they ever go home again, as I had been able to?* Tears ran down my cheeks. *I should be angry,* I thought, *but instead I just feel pity.*

* * *

Once we were settled, Mama went to look for the various people who had been kind to me during the war, even if only for a short time. She wanted to thank them for the role they had played, large or small, in protecting me. First she went to visit Mr. and Mrs. Ivanov, who had cared for me when I got sick in the ghetto. They were amazed to see that we had survived, and then revealed to us that they had suffered greatly that evening when they came home to find me gone. "There was no Feema!" Mrs. Ivanov said. "I thought I was going to die!" They told me how disappointed they were, and how they had hoped to finally have a daughter of their own. "But we did not know where to look for you!" Of course they could not have looked for me. They could not have even asked after me. That is what wartime was like.

Next we went to find Mrs. Podloska, in whose pantry I slept for the first two weeks that Mama left me behind. She had no idea what had happened to me once I left her house. She certainly did not know that in all those months, I had been sleeping under her house, keeping warm next to her dog! "How did you survive, Feema?" she asked me in amazement.

"I walked all around the streets during the day," I told her, "and at night I sometimes used to sleep in the cubbyhole right under your house."

"*My* house?" she said, puzzled and confused.

"Yes," I said. "Under *your* house next to *your* dog."

The woman's face became white and I thought she might faint. "I did what I could," she said, looking toward Mama. "But then I could not do anymore. I just could not."

"Of course," Mama said. And we both hoped Mrs. Podloska knew we were grateful for what she *had* done.

We also paid a visit to Mrs. Rozov, who had hidden me, fed me, and bathed me, letting me heal from the rash caused by the lice. Although I was only in her house for one week, I could never have survived if someone hadn't caught that infestation in time.

Yes, Mama and I thanked these people, then, and I still thank them now. To this day I bless them for their great and selfless deeds of kindness. It says in the *Torah*, our Jewish code for living, *if you save one life, it is as if you saved the whole world.*

13. WE START OVER

About one month later a letter arrived. Mama's heart rejoiced when she saw my brother David's handwriting on the envelope! In the letter, David said that he had survived the war, and he would soon be coming home. We had not seen him for four years! Now our family was almost whole again. Except for Papa...

Mama enrolled me in school. Although I was almost nine years old, I had never been to school so I was placed in the second grade. School was wonderful! Every day I wore a fresh white blouse and a navy blue skirt, proud to have the privilege of being a student. I was the only Jewish child in the class. The other Jewish children had either perished during the war or were safely off in other countries. I would never see those young people again.

During classes, I sat at a desk and listened to a teacher who taught all the lessons in Russian. I loved learning. I had waited for the chance to go to school and could not grasp the new knowledge fast enough! I looked forward to each day and vowed that someday I would grow up to be a teacher.

When I got home in the afternoon, I took good care of my school uniform, washing my blouse and ironing it for the next day. My uniform was precious to me, my best clothing. I only had one pair of good shoes – my short lace-up boots, and I did not want them to wear out. In order to preserve them, I *made* myself another pair of shoes. It was amazing to see how creative we were with so little. Scavenging in the bombed out houses, I collected rope. Gently pulling the strands of rope apart gave me a coarse thread. Mama taught me how to crochet the thread into soft shoes. When I was done, I placed a piece of cardboard inside to serve as an inner sole. My little rope shoes worked well, and when they wore out, I simply crocheted another pair.

People found many ways to survive after the war. Mama and Jeannie collected used army blankets to sell in the marketplace. They were out of the house for much of the day and only returned in the evening, so I had the job of scrubbing the floors, making the beds, and preparing potato soup. Many people in town were without homes, food, or jobs. Mama opened our home to anyone who did not have enough to eat or a place to sleep. We offered our hungry neighbors hot soup or fruit, and there was always the samovar with hot water for tea.

The war may have been over, but the problems were not. The new government was now investigating some of the events that took place in our town, and local people were being questioned about their actions. One day my mother got a call and learned that our friend Mr. Petrov, who had hidden us in his cellar and had fed me when I was hungry, had been arrested. He was being accused of refusing to help Jews during the war. There was going to be a hearing, and anyone who knew him was being called. That included us.

My mother took me to court to be a witness. I was just nine years old, but Mama knew that I could testify. In a circular, somber room, I was put on a chair and asked to speak about Mr. Petrov. The courtroom was filled with people who were listening eagerly. When I heard the court accuse this good man of having turned his head while others suffered, anger rose up in me. "How can you lie?" I said. "We were running for our lives! The Nazis were looking everywhere for us and this man took us in!" I described how kind he had been to my mother, my sister, and me, hiding us for a night in his cellar, and feeding me when I was alone and hungry in a cold city. "Without his help," I said angrily, "we would not be here today!" When I finished speaking, the people applauded. The accusations were withdrawn and Mr. Petrov was freed.

* * *

One day not long after that, the new city

government told us that another family would come to live with us. Although Mama was generous and had shared everything we had with other suffering people, she did not want to live this way again, for it reminded her of our days in the ghetto. She wanted to find a new way of life in another part of the world, wherever that might be. Anyway, there was no reason to stay in Europe. Almost everyone we loved and knew was gone.

The house was put up for sale. We were lucky because we got a buyer right away. Mama told him he would have to pay in gold, not in Russian rubles, the new currency. What would we do with rubles? Wherever we were going, no one was going to want rubles! And so the buyer paid Mama in gold coins. These would be what we would live on in the months, maybe years, to come, until we could find our scattered family members who could help us.

As always, Mama was *smart,* finding solutions to our many problems. She knew we had a long and dangerous road to travel, and we could not be seen carrying gold coins! But where and how could we hide them?

Mama had an idea. With the gold coins hidden under her coat, she took me to the cobbler. "Take off your boots, Feema," she said. I did. Then she took the boots from me and handing them to the cobbler along with the coins, she told him, "Open the soles and put these coins inside. Then close them up again." That was Mama's solution. With the gold in my boots, I would *walk* our money out of the country!

We left the cobbler's shop with the coins safely hidden in the bottom of my boots. Surely no one would ever suspect a child of being a smuggler! But how *heavy* those gold coins were! I walked as though I was a little old lady, slowly and with great effort, but I was never stopped or questioned. Once again, Mama had found a way to save us.

One day it was time to leave for good. "Children," Mama said, "say goodbye to our home." We walked out, taking nothing, not looking back. Our destination was a

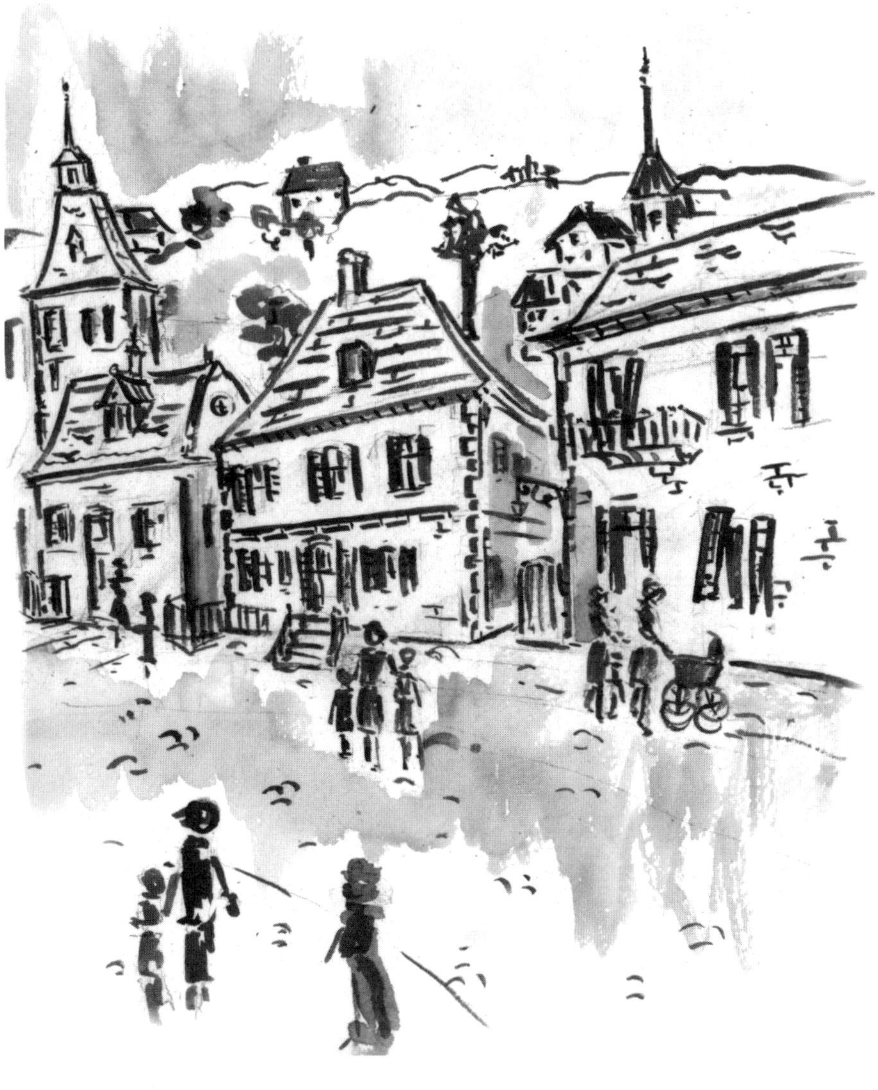

displaced persons camp in Germany, where we would try to connect with relatives who lived in America.

Like many other victims of the war, we took a train to the Ukrainian border. And by a series of small and sometimes dangerous miracles, we made it across that border into Germany, smuggled with other refugees in a military truck.

We did not know what lay ahead, but we had learned that despite all the horror we had seen and lived, there were good people everywhere. With their help and our own strength and courage, we could create a new life in a new place.

14. LEAVING EUROPE

It was several years before Mama, David, Jeannie and I reached our final destination. Our journey was a long one.

We stayed in the displaced persons camp for some time. In the camp, there were classes for children, and I tried to learn as much as I could. My education had been interrupted more than once, but I always loved school and longed to keep studying. Then we had to leave Germany because there was no future for us there.

We took a train that brought us from Germany to Paris, France. We were not going to live there. It was just a place to stay until we could get our papers to go to America. Aunt Elizabeth and Aunt Margaret, who lived in New York, were trying to arrange that for us.

A Jewish agency placed us in a rooming house right in the middle of Paris. With the ravages of war, the city had suffered, but its beauty shone through. There were wide boulevards and elegant buildings, just as we had had at home.

Since we did not expect to be in Paris very long, Mama did not enroll me in school. Instead, I busied myself doing charity work for unfortunate people, bringing food parcels to Moroccan families who were living in mountainside villages outside of Paris. I also volunteered as a "mother's helper," taking care of small children. And because I had quickly learned the layout of Paris and its subway system, the *metro*, I was able to accompany elderly people around the city on their doctor visits.

One day, Mama heard some news that frightened her – there was a rumor going around that World War III was about to start. "Oh, no!" Mama said. "We are not going to stick around for *that*! We are getting out of here right away."

Now we could not wait any longer for our

passage to America. We would have to go somewhere else – anywhere – as long as it was out of Europe. My Aunt Clara lived in Cuba, and Mama wrote to her, saying, *Get us out!* Somehow, Aunt Clara got together the money and the necessary papers to do this for us.

Then we made the big trip across the Atlantic Ocean. The boat left from Cannes, France and took us to Cuba, making various stops along the way. I had not seen the ocean too many times, and now I was *traveling* across it! It was thrilling and exhilarating, especially since we were going toward freedom.

It took three weeks to get to Cuba, and when we arrived on this small island, it was like coming to some kind of paradise! For us, leaving the ruins of Europe, Cuba was a beautiful, peaceful place where there was *nothing* to fear and *no one* to fear. Freedom at last.

Of course, none of us spoke a word of Spanish. Being so young and with such a hungry mind, I picked up the language in only three months! Then Aunt Clara enrolled me in a private school so I could go on with my education. I loved all the subjects – math, history, reading, and was even awarded a gold medal when I graduated from sixth grade. But more than studying, I loved having the honor of holding the Cuban flag in the morning assembly.

I was growing up and everything was starting to take shape. I was studying the piano again and began to enjoy the kind of life a young girl should have. Of course, a precious piece of all our lives would always be missing, for we never saw Papa again and could not find out what had become of him. But we had to go on despite that. Many people had lost their families. At least we were lucky enough to have the chance to begin again.

When I was just thirteen, I went out to work so that Mama would not have to work anymore. She had been through so much already and it was time for her life to become a little easier. I got a job at my cousin's shirt factory, where I worked during the day. At night I went to school because I had a goal. I wanted to be a teacher and knew that one day I would make this happen.

And it did. But perhaps I will save that for another story – the story of how I met my husband and had three beautiful children here in America, the most wonderful country in the world, and the place I gratefully and finally came to call **home**.

* * *

EPILOGUE

My story is just one of thousands that resulted from the devastation of the Second World War. Countless families like mine were displaced, communities broken apart, and an entire culture destroyed. This was the culture that was Jewish Europe ~ one of music, literature, art and history. Now it is gone.

But I consider myself among the most fortunate because I was able to leave Europe with at least part of my family. With everything I experienced, both good and bad, I never forgot my cousin Isac, my little companion from ghetto days. When I got married and had a child, I named him after Isac and his father (my uncle) in remembrance of these relatives whose lives ended tragically. They did not live to make the journey out of Europe, but like my Papa, they will always live in my heart.

We did rebuild our lives with will and determination in a new place, which we found right here. It is without hesitation that I say again and again, **G-d Bless America**, my new-found homeland.

Frima Laub, 2009